Apes!

**By Carol Harrison
Illustrated by Greg Harris**

Reviewed by Colleen McCann, Ph.D., Mammal Department,
Wildlife Conservation Society/Bronx Zoo.

© 1999 McClanahan Book Company, Inc.
All rights reserved.
Published by McClanahan Book Company, Inc.
23 West 26th Street, New York, NY 10010
ISBN: 0-7681-0180-8
Printed in the U.S.A.
10 9 8 7 6 5 4 3 2 1

They run and wrestle. They're very curious.
And they love to play just like you!

They're Apes!

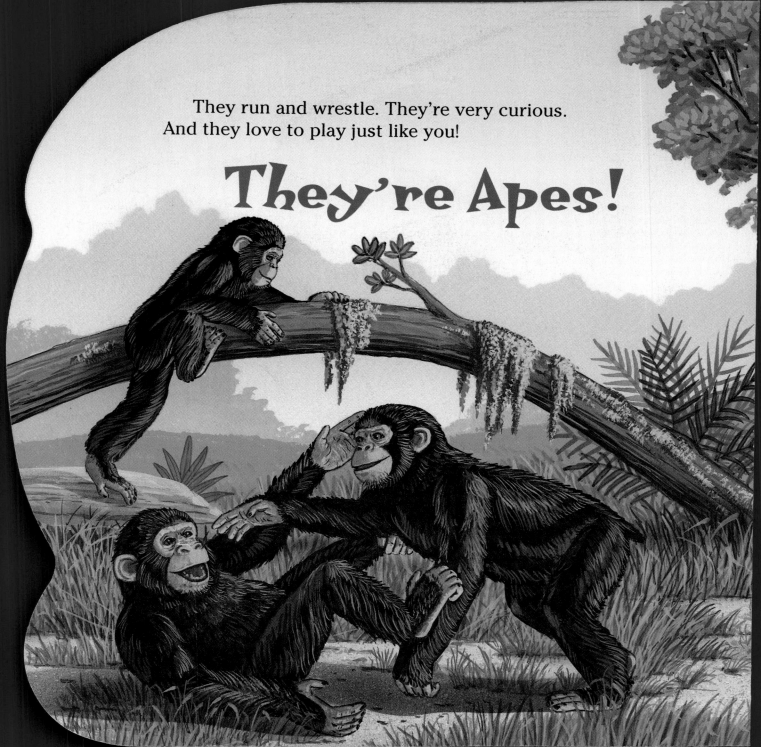

Five Kinds of Apes

gorilla orangutan chimpanzee bonobo gibbon

Amazing Apes

Apes are mammals—they are warm-blooded, have hair on their bodies, and the moms produce milk for their babies. Apes are called **primates** because they have a thumb that can press against the tips of their other fingers. This allows them to grasp and handle objects firmly.

leaf sponge

rock nutcracker

Monkeys have tails, apes don't!

termite stick

Besides humans, apes are the smartest primates.
They can learn to make and use simple "tools" to help get
food or water.

Gorillas

Gorillas are the largest and fiercest-looking apes, but they are gentle animals that rarely fight. A male gorilla only beats his chest to make a drumming sound that warns other gorillas to stay away from his troop!

Facts

Homeland
Forests of eastern and central Africa

Average weight
Female 157-215 pounds (71-98 kg)
Male 350-386 pounds (159-175 kg)

Fact
There are three different kinds of gorilla: the smaller western lowland gorilla, the eastern lowland gorilla, and the mountain gorilla.

Gorillas are **herbivores**, which means they mostly eat plants. An adult mountain gorilla may eat up to 45 pounds (20 kg) of plants a day—about as much as thirty heads of lettuce!

Chimpanzees

Chimpanzees live in large troops with fifty or more chimps of all ages. Individuals groom each other's fur to rake out dirt and insects. Grooming helps keep chimps clean, but more importantly it can show love for a friend or respect for a leader.

Chimpanzees usually travel on the ground. Like most apes, they have pads on their knuckles because they walk on all fours. Apes occasionally walk on two legs like people!

A male chimp can become a troop leader by screaming, waving branches, and charging until the other males back down!

Facts

AFRICA · ASIA
Atlantic Ocean · Indian Ocean

Homeland
Rainforests and dry grasslands of western to eastern Africa

Average weight
Female 70-100 pounds (32-45 kg)
Male 88-132 pounds (40-60 kg)

Fact
Chimpanzees are **frugivorous**. That means they mostly eat fruit. They also eat leaves, honey, insects, and sometimes small animals.

Bonobos

Bonobos are very affectionate with each other. They often kiss and hug, and seldom fight. Bonobos can make many different sounds, and the members of a bonobo troop "talk" to each other a lot, especially when looking for food.

Bonobo troops spend the day searching for food. They like to eat fruit and plants.

When bonobo males meet, they sometimes take turns making noises and repeating each other's sounds for several minutes. This is their way of getting to know a stranger or communicating with a member of their troop.

Facts

ASIA
AFRICA
Atlantic Ocean
Indian Ocean

Homeland
Central African rainforest

Average weight
Female 70 pounds (32 kg)
Male 85 pounds (39 kg)

Fact
All bonobos have the same "hairdo." Their black hair is parted naturally in the middle!

Orangutans

Orangutans spend most of their lives in trees. They are the slowest-moving apes. Big males sometimes have to travel on the ground because the tree branches can't support them!

Like most apes, they are frugivorous. Unlike the other apes, orangutans don't form groups. A mother travels with her baby, but otherwise orangutans live alone. Because they are alone and slow, smaller orangutans must watch out for clouded leopards that hunt high in the trees at night.

Facts

ASIA

Pacific Ocean

Indian Ocean

Homeland
Tropical forests of southeast Asia

Average Weight
Female 73-99 pounds (33-45 kg)
Male 176-200 pounds (80-91 kg)

Fact
Orangutan is a Malaysian word that means "person of the forest."

Gibbons

Gibbons spend nearly all their time in the treetops, swinging by their arms from branch to branch. This is called **brachiation**, and gibbons are the only apes that travel this way. They can swing through the treetops at 40 miles per hour (65 kmh).

Gibbons are the only apes that mate for life. They travel with their young in small family groups in search of fruit.

Facts

ASIA
Pacific Ocean
Indian Ocean

Homeland
Tropical forests of southeast Asia

Average weight
Female 10-19 pounds
(4.5-8.5 kg)
Male 11-22 pounds
(5-10 kg)

Fact
Gibbons are called lesser apes. They are smaller than all the other kinds of apes—which are known as great apes.

Ape Families

Gorillas, chimps, and bonobos live in large groups.
Gorilla troops usually follow the biggest, strongest male.

The leader of a chimp troop is often the loudest,
rowdiest male. Bonobos are the only apes in which
the females may share the responsibility of leading
the troop!

Most apes prefer to sleep in trees. At night they build sleeping nests by folding down branches and covering them with leaves and moss. Some gorillas, especially big ones, make their sleeping nests on the ground.

Gibbons are the only apes that don't build sleeping nests. They have padded bottoms, like built-in pillows, to rest on!

Baby Apes

Apes usually have one baby at a time because the infants need a lot of care and attention. They cling to their mothers' chests with their hands and feet for the first few months of life. After that, they are big enough to ride piggyback.

Gibbon fathers take an active role in raising their young—more than most other male apes do.

Baby apes learn to crawl and walk just as human babies do, only faster. Apes stay close to their mothers for up to five years, and they learn by watching the adults and by playing at "grown-up" things, such as making sleeping nests.

"Talking" Apes

Apes communicate with each other by gesturing and by making sounds. Primatologists, the scientists who study apes, can recognize more than thirty different sounds that chimps make to each other. Apes also communicate with facial expressions. What do you think these chimps are saying?

I'm afraid.

I'm excited.

I'm angry.

Primatologists have taught some apes to "speak" in sign language. Apes can't talk like people—they don't have the voice muscles and short tongues needed to form the words and sounds that humans make.

Bet You Didn't Know . . .

Apes can learn to solve problems!

Apes can hold and manipulate objects with their feet almost as well as they can with their hands.

Apes have exactly the same number of teeth as humans—32!

Apes can learn to paint pictures, look at picture books, and play computer games!

One of the first U.S. astronauts was a chimpanzee named Enos! In 1961, he spent 16 minutes in a space capsule orbiting Earth.

Koko, a trained gorilla in a research center, used sign language to ask for her own pet kitten. She named it All Ball!

Apes are inquisitive and intelligent creatures. People love to watch and study them. And who knows, they may be watching and studying us!